About the Author

Laurnene lives alone near Tucson, Arizona where she presently assists with her parents. She loves good humour and tends to be optimistic and down to earth. A 'kid at heart', she likes adventure and will take every opportunity to travel. In her free time you'll find her either volunteering with the State Parks, hiking, fishing or visiting friends or family.

Dedication

I dedicate this book to my wonderful daughters who I love dearly
and continue to be thoroughly amazed by.

Laurnene D. Frey

THE GAY DEPRESSION

AUSTIN MACAULEY
PUBLISHERS LTD.

A CIP catalogue record for this title is available from the British Library.

ISBN 9781785542336 (Paperback)
ISBN 9781785542343 (Hardback)
ISBN 9781785542350 (E-Book)

www.austinmacauley.com

First Published (2016)
Austin Macauley Publishers Ltd.
25 Canada Square
Canary Wharf
London
E14 5LQ

Contents

Preface

This book was mainly comprised during my years in the Navy before the "don't ask, don't tell..." policy; back in the days when no one in the U.S. would dare mention living a LGBT lifestyle.

Thankfully, the progress made over the last few decades has had far-reaching effects, helped along by those in the publics' eye who have stood up and said, "This is who I am."

My heartfelt thanks to those who have fought for freedom and equality for us all.

A special note to the reader:

I wish to share several of *my* truths that I have learned over the years…

1. Friends stand by their friends; <u>always</u>.
2. If one is only kind where kindness and respect are returned, then their efforts are surely not genuine; nor is the love they present, "unconditional". Expectations of any kind must only be met within yourself.
3. The battle is hard won, but one should never be less than who they are. What integrity is there in that?
4. Love and adversity are tools. It is through them we learn much and begin to understand and accept our own inner strengths and peace.
5. Right and wrong are rigid and yet, "fashionable" concepts!

The following pages reflect dark, soul-searching days of self-acceptance. One need not be gay/lesbian to relate, for social injustice is not a limited hatred. Nor is the path of self-discovery confined to one lifestyle.

For those who find themselves in similar pain and/or confusion, I hope my efforts will reassure them that that are not alone… and that a cold distrusting heart is no way to survive.

1. Birth

BEGINNINGS

Beginnings-
> Warm
> > Secure
> > > Envelopment...
> > Drifting in a silent sea...

Quiet
> Peaceful
> > Alone –
> Growing with a feeling ...
> > Of
> > > Belonging –

BIRTH

Birth –
       Aching, cramping
        Trapped –
       Pain, darkness…
        Gasping for breath –
Light –
       Piercing blindness
        Relentless surging seas…
Drowning –
       In an endless
        Void
           Of comfort…
Struggling;
       --alone.

DOOR-PRIZE

Words,
        Words…
Mouths moving – saying nothing
Needing,
        Searching
        "Listen!"
Seeing,
        Feeling
        "Obey!"
Looking,
        Reading; must learn
        "Don't Bother Me!"
Touch me –
        Hear me –
        "See My Child!"
Trophies –
        … a door prize
        Don't put me
        On your shelf
        …I don't belong –
         But,
           Where?

AN AUTUMN LEAF

Feel the colors surge through my veins!
        Brilliant splashes of light!
Red here,   orange there…
        With just a streak of yellow.

I am bold.
I am unique.

My friend the wind plays with me –
        First a gentle caress;
Then suddenly as if with a sense
        Of urgency,

Whips me free from the limb and playfully,
        Tenderly floats me to the ground.
There, in that brief moment in time,
        I am free of all bonds but the soft guidance of my dear friend.

I quiver with sheer joy
        Until I finally come to rest
On the damp earth
        With my brothers and sisters.

We've painted the forest floor
        With the brilliance of our passing…
Eventually to fade, and change once again
        In an effort to nurture the young leaves yet to blossom.

2. I'm not "Gay" I'm "Tortured"

THE TROUBADOUR

Ah… the troubadour of tragic comedy –
    My life unveils
    Laughter clothed in tears.

The chorus
    All can sing
    No surprise's the verses bring.

Audiences applaud
    (His) foolish ventures
    Jester blind to lovers masks.

Oh, to march to a different drummer…
    -Too late-
    The die is cast.

THE QUESTION

"You look at me and I hurt inside. Do you?
        And if you do –
        Why?
And if you can tell me why –
        Will you?"
The years have not changed the hurt –
        It's there, if not more painful
Than yesterday's bitter tears.

You look at me and I die. Do you?
        And, if we do – why?
And if I knew
        Would you listen?

PERCEPTIONS

I'm starving –
> But my stomach is too swollen to eat.

I'm tired –
> But I'm too weary to sleep.

I want –
> But I know not what for.

My eyes are blurry
> From trying to see…
>> To find…

My hands are blistered
> From trying to hold on
To some semblance of reality.

Where others walk the paved road of life
> And trip over its occasional pitfalls
Kicking the pebbles out of their way

I swim alongside;
> Sometimes catching one of two of the discarded pebbles…
Finding an entire world therein.

THE STARVING MAN

I am not unlike the starving man who,
Upon crawling to the edge of an expansive
Bluff finds himself overlooking the Sultan's feast.

As he longingly gazes at festivities he knows he could never join,
The bluff crumbles and he crashes down
Into the center of activities;

His nostrils/senses flooded with the delicious,
Penetrating odors of the delicacies he had
Just been admiring…

His needs are overwhelming – but denied.

He is too weak to leave his tormenting surroundings…
Nor is he willing to try.

His stomach convulses –
He is too proud to beg…
Too empty to cry.

The pain he holds must remain his own;
A burden he carries to his death…
An uneventful event of re-joining the desert sands and
The arid desert winds…

But the pain remains –
A tortured soul is
Eternal.

THE REMAINS OF THE DAY

"…The answers must come from inside
           Hold and nurture the parts that are hurting
           Trust the process
           You won't always be alone…"

I've heard it all… and as I hold myself and gently rock
           The tears cascade…
Wearing a deep chasm of grief through my soul

Exposing vital organs that relentlessly refuse to be still –
           Never any peace…

Waiting to be splayed before the next curious player
           Erosion continues
A grotesque display…
           The remains of the day.

EYES

...eyes;
        Wide, deep
Helplessly searching
        For answers –
Their misery tears deep
        Into my own emptiness.

The children of the world
        - Continuously waiting;
And trying to discover
        What they wait for.

We all reach out to one another –
        Or to anything we can grasp
As we wander farther
        And farther through the days, hours and minutes of our lives –
Each with our own measured
        Amount of useless searching

The sea is some comfort –
        Perhaps something familiar to us
Many eons ago
        Caresses our tortured souls
As they merge with the crashing surf and
        Drift high into the swirling blue vastness of the skies

Only then do we
        Curl our toes
Deep into the wet sand
        Reminding us once again
Of particles and pieces –
        And endless time...

LAKE OF TEARS

Solitary, isolated
        Lake of tears –
Private, guarded
        A chance discovery –

Clear, perfect reflections
        On a mirrored surface
Images;
        Capturing fleeting emotions…
Quiet, silent
        Admiration –
Suddenly,
        Unexpected movements

Accidental intrusion
        Into hidden waters
Surface tensions
        Disturbed…

Perimeters convulse
        Visions blur; distort…
Realities remain constant –
        Reflections no longer clear, recognizable –

Time passes…
        Waters reveal few secrets…
Our tears meld
        With the crystal blue waters –

And carry prayers
        Of someday
Swimming freely within
        Its depths.

ALONE/TOGETHER

You say you are one who remains
        Lonely…
            Within a crowd –
The desperate hours of hoping
        And
            Bitter searching...

How well I know them.
Your thoughts embrace my soul
        And
            It cries out to you in return
… Has a moment yet passed?

I see the end
        Of uncertainties –
        Questioning –
…but it too, is merely a beginning

The splendor, the joy, the warmth
        That awaits…

My answers lie deep within your eyes –
        …the fire of your touch
As we melt into one.

I have but scratched the surface
        Save the crowd, 'we are' –
        And yet
'We' does not fit…

'We' is the static energy
        Merging from our fingertips as we draw close
…must I explain?

Reach me –
        …we cannot touch.
Think of me –
        …we shall be bound.

We shall be living
        Alone/together within a crowd.
…tomorrow we may touch.

THE PRAYER

Please God,
>Help me to believe –
>Help me to have faith and strength –

Why God,
>Why do we doubt?
>…our own insecurities, perhaps
Doubting others through our doubt in ourselves?

Which can I say is better, God –
>At one time I never knew my other half –
Therefore,
>I only longed and searched for the unknown…

Now you present her to me, God –
>But she is out of reach.
The ache of knowing
>And not being able to join
As the one we are intended to be.

Then,
>We doubt –
>We cry –
>We love…

God, give us both the strength –
>Please, God…
>Let me believe.

TREASURED MOMENTS

Time –
        Friend and enemy…
Eternally slow –or-
        Devastatingly swift
Teasing –or- enveloping

'Your time' –
        Limited, for me…
Elusive yet alluring glimpses
Of the glimmering richness, flash before my eyes –
        Always beyond reach…
        Never to be mine (?)

Ah, those moments –
        Such bliss.
        But never without reservation.
The full glory only to be felt
        When I know the treasure to be mine;

Then time becomes my constant loving partner
        And I am at peace.

EVOLUTION OF THE RAIN

Life flows on hand in hand with time –
          Constantly moving/changing.

Like rain, it gathers up gradually
             And grows from pieces gathered here and there
Till it is so weighted down
          It takes 'form';

For just a short time it may be seen
           As it falls back to the earth
And shatters into a million pieces
          Once again.

Life, rain;
          Both similar…
Funny –
          Rain and tears are similar too.

3. The irritation of listening to words different than those we want to hear –
One should talk to himself if opinions other than his own are so distasteful to his palate.

"The growth of intimacy is like that. First one gives off his best picture, the bright and finished product mended with bluff and falsehood and humor. Then more details are required and one paints a second portrait, and a third – before long the best lines cancel out – and the secret is exposed at last; the planes of the pictures have intermingled and given us away, and though we paint and paint we can no longer sell a picture. We must be satisfied with hoping that such fatuous accounts of ourselves as we make to our wives and children and business associates are accepted as true".

The Beautiful and Damned by F. Scott FitzGerald

THE EXECUTIONERS EMBRACE

Your reality [of me] –
        Merely a fabricated pretense
Of your own creation.

A contrived evolution from
        The veracity of
Our eyes first whispers…

To the iron gripped resolve
        Of the executioners
Hooded embrace.

You, my judge/my jury –
        Yet never
Were my words "heard".

The resounding word
        "Guilty" reverberates loudly
Within the narrow confines of your world.

Is this your comfort?
Truly, what threat do I present?

To care is not to pity…
        Tho 'tis a pity
That kindness would trigger
        Such defense, reconnaissance… despair.

I choose not to participate
        In the follies of your mind.
Therein lies no battle for me…
In that intercourse
        Lie only the skeletons of
Hope and compassion.

Better for me
        To delight in warm shadows
Of faded memories.

To draw in
        The resins left from when
Two souls let their hearts first touch.

Before unkind words
        And distrust
Smear the innocence of the moment.

PERCEPTIONS II

Did you ever notice that
We see what we want to
In others –
And sometimes
We see "others" in
Everyone…

...TO COMMUNICATE

Words may be a 'tool' we
Would all be better off without –

Such an awkward substitute
For communication
          The soul cannot reach out
          And envelope with words –

One cannot share a life-force
With words – and seeing a
Lack of explanation is left, abandoned –

-Mechanical robotics existence-

Energy dissipates when not tapped...
...remember, how to 'Feel'?

All is equated to sexual
Involvement – how limiting.

Vast expansions of awareness
Left to be forgotten
          Dust to dust
The knowledge crumbles –

SWEET LADY DECEIT

Ah – Sweet Lady Deceit…

May she one day trip over
Her own wicked tongue and
Lay quiet in the slime
Of the gutters she has created.

ONWARD CHRISTIAN SOLDIERS

Onward Christian Soldiers
        Cause your brothers strife
Change him to your lifestyle –
        Or end his life

Elevate your soul
        By standing on his body
You know what's right –
        You know 'His' word –

You pass judgment…
        Save 'Him' the work –
'Born Again'… without 'sin'
        You place your self-righteousness above *The Lord* –

Beware…
        You walk a blind alley.

4. Man can easily deal with man –
It's his soul
That gets in the way

MORNING MEDITATIONS

The silence of the early morning is deafening
   It seems only to amplify the aching in my heart.
I am intensely aware of being alone –
   And extremely lonely.

The clock and I sit and wait as the minutes of time
   Slowly tick by
Each of which contain a lifetime
   Together we are alone.

We wait and watch as the sun
   Slowly yet mechanically rises
And sheds her light –
   A new day begins.

SURVIVAL

Survival...
>A funny concept –
What we do to keep our spirits going
>Often times prevents us from living.

Compassion...
>Plenty for others –
What of myself? How to balance
>Self-care and friend-care.

Control...
>Emotional –
Control –or– care when beyond
>Ourselves.

Fear...
>The big juice –
I'm tired of hurting
>I wish to play the game from the safety of the base-lines.

Isolation...
>Is the only way
To get through my
>Fears, control, compassion and 'Survive'?

--how lonely
--how sad

HIDE AND SEEK

...the movement of the wind –
        It whispers
"Move with me"...
        It shouts to
"Find me"...

Find me –
        I must find myself.
Should I run with the wind?
        It is ever constant.

Enveloping me within its strong arms –
        Sometimes gentle
        Sometimes cruel and harsh.

Still at times I wonder,
        Is it there –
And it is; ever constant...

Where can I go
        To hide from it –
Or shall I...
"Move with me"...
        It whispers to
Find me...
        Find me...

THE TEAR

The ink smears
And runs down the page
Combining the rigid lines of acceptance
With the chanced and hurried flares of fantasy –

Both blended into a watered down stream
Of color…
Dull and meaningless
In their union

Abandoned and unable to decipher
They are left alone…
The gaze of the casual onlooker
May resemble that of a half-blind man

Desperately trying to focus
On an oil slick
Gathered by the mists and rains
Of an early fall morning –

Colors and contours of
No special dimension but
With the depth and the soul
Of time itself

There's so much to be seen –
And yet
No one
To interpret the meanings

THE THIEF

I want to hide
But cannot rise
Lord, save me from those dreadful eyes
They're blind you see
They cannot feel
   And yet
They're sure they saw me steal…

They cut me wide
They prod inside
They say I have no soul…
Dear God it hurts –
   I love them so
   I never thought I stole

They come again
They take my heart
They say my soul is dead –
'Of course', say I, through bitter tears
Now one less thing to dread –
To save it from your angry tread
I slaughtered it instead.

SERPENT

My serpent lies within
    My chest –
Entwining
    Encircling
        Embracing my heart

Tenderly caressing
    -then-
Threatening to crush the
    Life from me, only
Always to
    Stop short…

You are my temptation
You are my forbidden fruit –
    Oh how you glisten and
        Shine with an
            Inner radiance
Mesmerizing to the eye
    Captivating to the soul
        Compelling to my death…

The serpent writhes within my skin
    But
I mustn't let you see –
    You mustn't know
The force and character of such a
    Beast as mine would certainly
Frighten you away…
    Away,
Farther than the vast expanses which
    I longingly gaze across now.

5. Death...

"...And the conversation rises and slowly fades into silence
And you see behind every face the mental emptiness deepen
Leaving only the growing terror of nothing to think about;
Or when under ether, the mind is conscious but conscious of nothing –

I said to my soul, be still, and wait without hope
For hope would be hope for the wrong thing; wait without love
For love would be love of the wrong thing; there is yet faith
But the faith and the love and the hope are all in the waiting.
Wait without thought for you are not ready for thought:
So the darkness shall be the light, and the stillness the dancing."...

T.S. Eliot

HIDDEN DANGERS

Spring brings forth
>> The fragrant blossoms
>> Of color…

So dearly missed
>> After the harshness
>> Of winter

Longing with
>> Unquenched desire
>> One often forgets…

The loveliest of flowers
>> The sweetest
>> Of nectars…

Often harbors
>> The most poisonous
>> Of thorns.

THE OFFENSIVE EYE

Years ago, yet merely months
        My eye offended me –
I plucked it out.

Now and forever I am forced to wander
        Half-blind, half-in-darkness –
Searching to cure my wounds.

For in my rashness I did not notice
        The offender was not my eye at all –
Indeed, it was but a small particle
        Of dust hidden within.

ROSES

Red flagged petals of desire; (someone else's)
Fading and dropping --- as the tears of my un-stilled
anguish...

The tenderness tears at my heart
A heart which remains bound in thorny vines...

I bleed ---
The mere pulsing of my heart impales it on poisonous barbs...
Pull at the bindings
And, I suffer avulsions...
Cut at the encasements
And, inevitable cut deeper into an already damaged soul.

Anxiously I wait for the vines to die
Allowing the scars to heal...

But the roots feed deeply –
Far too deeply...
Sending new shoots into every nerve/extremity ---

I move my fingers
And, the motion is felt in my gut –
I see you
And, agony blurs my vision –
I silently reach for you (always you turn away)...
Foolishly, the ache prevails ---
Vines remain green... and strong.

My tears well up inside
And begin to escape...
The only thing to be set free –
The salt-waters of my soul spill red...
And I, the only one to be stained ---

The corpse of my soul;
Hidden/obscured –
Entwined in thorny remnants which have
Sapped the very life from me –

The new roses grow red...
But nothing else remains.

BLOOD PATTERNS

Blood patterns swim
>Grief spills and distorts the image…

Pretty, artistic
>The ability to change and yet always belong…

How wonderful!
>Ever-changing and yet always defined…

Pain racks my cold, removed heart –
>You may see only part of me…

The mask is not a lie
>Only a very limited view, hiding the full person

Stay back –
>Just stay back…

FALSE HOPE

God –
        To live in fear…
I'm not very strong.

Feet have trampled me-
        Worms and insects bore at my roots and bark.

Storms have ripped at me –
        It's so hard… but I keep trying…
I know I'll make it.

You see
        Through it all
There still remains a leaf on my broken limbs.

See how green
        And new –

…why did it just fall?

INTERLUDES

Repress pain by feeling anger...
          Can't see the forest for the trees.

There are times when we know what we perceive to be real is so...
          No amount of denial can change that

I feel I have been an interesting interlude
          A lark... a past-time
I have learned much. I value the lessons.

Time is the ultimate controller...
          It brings our souls to bear witness to the harsh realities of
An immortal hell.

To see you, briefly...
          Touch you through endless life-times
And never to be allowed to be with you... timing always wrong.

We learn
          We grow...
When will it end?

You know who you need
          Your story is not ended with her.
Denial only intensifies the desire
          And condemns other relationships.

Allow yourself the love
          Allow yourself the companionship.

We will meet again
          I will know you;
How many years down the road, but...
          Will the time ever be right?

Now again,
          I die for you...
My tortured soul lives on.

ICE

Clothe me
> My body aches from the cold

All is ice –
> The minds
> The touch

I am numb to the crying…
> Was there really a tear?

Help me someone
> Help me God –
> Both intangible but
> Yet as one.

Do you dare ask of me?
> Do you remove the crumbs
> From a starving man's reach?

Leave me
> If I freeze I will feel less

Kiss me now
> I am gone

DEPRESSION

Many times have I felt this sense of awareness –
         Of being so alone…
I've been fighting off slipping into
         The depths of depressions now for quite a while.
Now, however, I feel myself reaching
         Trying to cling to the smooth, slimy walls
Of that eternal pit.
Fighting to keep myself from being
         Engulfed in that vast darkness.

God help me!
         My fingers ache from the endless groping –
I can feel myself sinking
         Not again… please

Not now… NO!

My stomach is in constant convulsions
         My head throbs harshly with every heartbeat.
My eyes are so tired of straining
         To see
         To find
         To understand…

My body is weak
         Don't let me slip into the darkness of depression again
It's so hard to find your way back out
The lights just went out…
         How ironic.

ELUSIVE EMOTIONS

We wander aimlessly through life
> Searching for the welcome sense of belonging –
Very few of us ever find
> The comfort and solitude gained from inner peace.

Death is such a feared reality
> We seldom face its presence
Yet there is peace and silent understanding attainable
> From our dead brothers and sisters.

What wisdom they must hold
> Deep within their final casing.
Their bodies in time, deteriorate and
> Their very souls reach out to teach.

To guide us in our blunderings
> But in this mortal life
We seldom if ever remove our protective
> Individual walls.

To give or receive any emotions
> We are so afraid of being ourselves.
We are so unknown…
> Do we seek to destroy what we could possibly be?

Is true emotion so foreign to us
> That we must always run and hide
If only from ourselves?

DEAD AND BURIED

I've been dead and buried now for months
You won't remember my name, but I know yours quite well.
I used to speak them often –
But that was yesterday, long before today –
Before I died.

I've been dead and buried now for months.
But you haven't noticed.
My smile was but a reflection;
A ghost in your eyes.
My voice merely a vague whisper carried in the breeze.

I've been dead and buried now for months.
But you didn't realize I was leaving.
Even though you helped bury me.
Yes, your words, broken promises, false hopes –
They're all here too.

I've been dead and buried now for months.
But you shouldn't feel badly.
If you ever want to see me
Just think of my smile and its shadow may appear –
After all, that's all I ever was; a shadow.

I've been dead and buried now for months
I wonder what it's like to have substance –
To have meaning or purpose.
Only in re-birth
Shall I know.

I've been dead and buried now for months
But you haven't noticed yet
Even though
I'm gone.

BRASS RINGS

Here lies the broken shell of a man –
        Composed of linked brass rings
Now tarnished with time
        And bits of colored glass.

Now reflecting haphazardly
        Off the jagged edges.

He was once whole –
        Shaped with the hands of birth
Destroyed now
        With the games of life.

CASTLES IN THE TIDES

My mind grow numb
My heart grows cold –
The lost love lies empty
        Of hopes and dreams…
Desires of the ego
        Lost in reality.

What now to hope for
When the sands of
        Decades sift swiftly away –
Not a grain to cling to.

All just castles in the tides…
        Too tired to build…
        No ideas left to construct.
        –Empty–

DARKNESS

Thorns of regret encase my soul…
        Entwine my heart.
Life-blood pours freely with
        Every movement
Wounds cause deep clinging mire
        Which immobilizes any progress from these self-made bonds.
Freedom is impossible…
        A distant shelter in the night.

The clouds clear
        Illuminating a spectacular galaxy far in the distance…
Oh to reach those heights
        Even the unknown would be better than this (?)
Doubt and fear close in…
        Blackness prevails once again.

6. Indeed,
The Phoenix will rise
For those
Who hear the beat
of their own
Drummer!

"People are often unreasonable, illogical, and self-centered; forgive them anyway. If you are kind, people may accuse you of selfish, ulterior motives; be kind anyway. If you are successful, you will win some false friends and some true "enemies"; succeed anyway. If you are honest and frank, people may cheat you; be honest and frank anyway. What you spend years building, someone could destroy overnight; build anyway. The good you do today, people will often forget tomorrow; do good anyway. Give the world the best you have, and it may never be enough; give the world the best you've got anyway. You see, in the final analysis, it is between you and God; it was never between you and them anyway."

Mother Theresa

BEING IN YOUR EMOTIONS

Being in your emotions…
        Funny, you think you are –
But then something happens
        And you realize you've only acknowledged
And denied them.

Confusion…

Over should, coulds, woulds…
        'Ifs' just don't cut it.

It's okay to be wherever I am
        Here and now
No explanations.

I didn't say I have to like it…
        Just be there.

Trying hard to not feel
        Trying to change feelings…
It won't work.

I still get angry because I am not
        "in control" of my emotions.
But, emotions are spiritual
        Not intellectual.

Spiritual things in life
        Must be acknowledged
Must be honored,
        So why don't I honor my own spirituality?

Who cares if I'm condemned for caring
        Is loving so wrong?
But self-care must enter into the process…
        Again, the balance.

THE LESSON

My body shivers
        Ignoring the suns futile attempts to warm this barren earth…
Barren? Well, perhaps not
        For those who have the unique gift of drawing life out of dust
Or response from cold, eroding cement.

We learn limits in class
        Do they never apply to life?

Negative
        Always fault…
Impress me someone
        Impress me with your trivial chatter.

Teach me more about how corrupt
        And apathetic we all are.
People all so intent on "living life and being real"…
        I wonder if they could recognize themselves.

Keep talking people, I'm listening
        But pardon if I only use half an ear.
There must be something I'm missing
        I focus most of my attention to you (there) so I won't miss it.

Unfortunately, I've heard all that you've said or possibly may say
        Many, many times.
I await for a possible mistake on your part…
        The sun is beginning to warm my feet.

THE VISION

Emotions run deep –
        Beyond know measure.
What have we to equate the intensities?
        The calms…

Surging, writhing, boiling masses of magma
        Intent on release –
The peaceful moments; silent, still…
        Dew clad as if kissed by angels, just before dawn.

These and more…

I feel so removed; so alien from my human counterparts
        So alone –
As if I must function on a separate plain…
        But to what purpose?

I drink and numb the difference –
        So strange, so unreal…
And where do you fit in?
        Somewhere in between, but just out of reach.

How I long to embrace you
        Yet dare not touch
Lest the 'image' be destroyed
        In the convergence zone.

I must walk my path… but at times,
        I seek your vision –
Embrace it to my heart
        And I can smile.

METAMORPHOSIS

The turbulent winds and seas
        Are the messengers of change
The deliverers of information.

It is during the times of calm waters
        That the metamorphosis takes place.

The processing of information into knowledge
        Knowledge to wisdom
And growth takes place.

The aura glows peaceful
        With renewed radiance.

THE GARDENER

Gardening –
        Pruning…
Cutting away the old glories
        And the damaged limbs so that new growth is promoted.

The plant would live without the nurturing hand
        Only, growth would retard…
The plant become weaker due to wasted energies
        Sent to the wrong places.

Cherish the memories of the past spring's blossoms
        But cut away their skeletons when it is summer.

Don't dwell on the years when the trees bare no fruit
        Or the locust destroyed what was developing.

Nurture and tend to the present season.

YOUR ANSWERS WILL COME FROM THE SEA

Your answers will come from the sea…

The wind is fierce… seagulls riding the air currents –
        What is it I'm here to learn?
What am I supposed to do?

Observe to learn and teach by example
        Love, honor, joy, integrity…
Pass on what you learn of life.

The gulls, scavengers that they are
        Have as much grace and beauty as the mighty eagle
While soaring on the breezes… who is boastful enough to negate ones'
purpose over another?

Don't fight the energies that carry us
        The birds rise and fall, maintain effortless flight for hours
Or they fight the currents, tire and fail…
        Falling far short of their desired goals; so we must not fight
the life force that carries us.

Treasure on the shore
        A bottle, shattered glass, polished fragments gathered for
adornments
All part of an evolutionary process; carried to distant, foreign shores.
        Time is the director, life the stage.

Growth and change our destiny
        All stages have their charred, painful periods, but
The process must be allowed to play out for the
        Knowledge to reflect in the product of that level… and then,
something new.

Agates among common dull rock
        But you must look closely, and want to find the
Beauty of the uncommon, unpolished gem stone.
        Where do our lives meet the shore?

Today the sea is active, churning
        Restless and determined.
But there is much to be learned when the wind is silent – becalmed.
        Only when stagnation sets in does death loom.

REALITY

The energies run freely
   For those who would tap
   Into the flow…

So easy where there is no
   Interference to avoid –

Which be the real world?
   Which be reality?

I perceive them both to 'be'

One; of basic life force energies…
One' of man- made directives.

One needed for the soul…
One necessary to survive in the physical realm we have created.

Balance is always the question –
   Balance, boundaries, limits.

One weighs more for me—
   I need my spirit to be far stronger
To survive the physical
   Demands of our man-made realities.

My spirit must know no restraints—
   This is a difficult boundary within
   Our un-chosen fates.

VISIONS OF THE PAST

Visions of the past...
        Subconscious images, refusing to rest;
        And yet, feelings evolve.

Compassion never fails me...
        This is good – my heart is not so hard;
        And yet the mind of daily reality is cold, angry and guarded.

Aging of the image...
        The pain and discomfort are theirs;
I offer comfort,
        But have released myself from other emotional entanglements.

Seeing past the mask...
        Learning to remove my own blinders;
        The lesson is good.

My physical back is turned...
        Now to emotionally walk away.

BALANCE

The pendulum hangs silent...
        Periods of stagnation or
        Peace and balance.

Change... growth.

The pendulum is drawn back fiercely to
        Begin splaying through its course.

Information gathers at both ends
        Bright and shiny like brass rings on one end;
        Solid unmoving survivor on the other.

One, illusionary happiness
        The other, warrior protection.

Slices...

Of life, love and emotions
        Are cut loose with every pulse
        Until the period of growth is played through.

The pendulum slows...
        And balance is once again achieved.

THE MATE

The lone wolf cries –
        The sound pierces the stillness of the night…
His soul screams out, begging the moon
        To illuminate his love –
           His mate –
           His destiny…

Shadows,
        Only tease his flesh as with each foot fall,
His angst and trepidation mount

She is close, but where"
        He calls… once again
Agony ripping deep from
        Within his chest –

He senses her presence
        She is there…
Only in her eyes
        Does he know the well of eternity…
The Spring of Life –

THE JOURNEYS END

It was the time of spring
        Of youthful energies
Of life's renewal, pushing through
        The harsh casings of winter

Colors emerging
        Hinting of hidden richness within –
How we danced in that joyous
        Excitement of discovery!

Too quickly the summer
        Carried our steps
Far from that promise of
        Emerging beauty

Far from the
        Nurturing love
And fascination
        Our innocence had fostered…

It was the time of fall
        A time of quiet reflection –
Suddenly the light fragrance
        Of something familiar

Filling our senses with
        A memory –
Bringing a smile so
        Sweet…

Though the blossom
        Was unknown to us,
The deepest part of our
        Soul remembers…

And with it
        A comfort –
And realization
        Of finally coming home.

SELENE

'She'
In all her infinite majesty;
Her star-studded grace,
        Beauty and love…

'She'
Who paints our dreams
With a gentle wave of
        Her hand…

Who opens our
Night-vision to the
        Vastness of the universe…

'She'
Who unfolds the
Mystery of life itself…

Even "she'
Cannot match
The unbridled force
Which grips my heart
        In the stillness of night –

When Selene
Brings me visions
        Of you.

ATLANTIS

I don't know why
        The sea –
The magical enchantment
        Of an elusive mermaid…

What of Atlantis'
        Majestic colonnades
Leading us
        To where…

She leads us
        Into the unknown
Depths of
        Our souls –

Uncharted pathways
        Interconnecting the
Sands of time…

For time is no
        Stranger to us
Though always short…

Here in the oceans
        Of my heart
Time seems to
        Stand still…

Only a shimmer, a ripple
        Then,
we are gone.

ETERNAL VOW

Let me touch you
        Embrace you
Within my soul

Let us join hands
        And weave magic
Around the strands of destiny

Each segment
        Of individual strength

Entwined with fate;
        A braid
Of eternal force

Let our energies
        Move through
The fingers of time and space

And together
        My love
Glow with the force only
        The creator can know.

MY FRIEND

My friend; she stands proudly in the bright sunlight basking in its glow
        Radiating its warmth back to anyone who would see…
But they see nothing but darkness as the sun's ray's shine from behind her
and not directly on them.

My friend; offering her hand to those who would reach out and take it…
But the effort is too much for them

My friend; a beautiful soul whose steps leave an iridescent shimmer
wherever she goes…
But they see only distorted shadows and refuse to look beyond to see her
true image

My friend; she feels their reproach to her core.
She would run from the sun, hiding in the darkness… removing herself
from judgment, the distinctness of her being blurring into nothingness…
allowing them to destroy her beauty through their own ignorance

My friend; I see you.

My friend; I will take your hand and remove you from the cold shadows
of obscurity for they do not provide the safety you would seek.

My friend; I will encourage you to stand once again in the dawning light
of day…
Away from those who would drag you down into their cold, darkened
reality – for it is not yours, and their visions are but their own

My friend; do not despair… for you are not alone